newprovidence
MEMORIAL LIBRARY

377 Elkwood Avenue
New Providence, NJ 07974

Fun Food for Cool Cooks

Grilled Pizza Sandwich

AND OTHER VEGETARIAN RECIPES

by Kristi Johnson

Capstone press

Mankato, Minnesota

Snap Books are published by Capstone Press,
151 Good Counsel Drive, P.O. Box 669, Mankato, Minnesota 56002.
www.capstonepress.com

B+T 18.95 9/08

Library of Congress Cataloging-in-Publication Data
Johnson, Kristi.
    Grilled pizza sandwich and other vegetarian recipes / by Kristi Johnson.
    p. cm. — (Snap books. Fun food for cool cooks)
    Summary: "Provides fun and unique vegetarian recipes including grilled pizza sandwiches,
easy cheesy potatoes, and spaghetti salad. Includes easy instructions and a helpful tools glossary with
photos" — Provided by publisher.
    Includes bibliographical references and index.
    ISBN-13: 978-1-4296-2018-5 (hardcover)
    ISBN-10: 1-4296-2018-8 (hardcover)
    1. Vegetarian cookery — Juvenile literature. I. Title. II. Series.
TX837.J54235 2009
641.5'636 — dc22   2008001763

Editor: Kathryn Clay
Designer: Juliette Peters
Photo Stylist: Sarah L. Schuette

Photo Credits:
All principle photography in this book by Capstone Press/Karon Dubke
Capstone Press/TJ Thoraldson Digital Photography, cooking utensils (all)
Tami Johnson, 32

1 2 3 4 5 6 13 12 11 10 09 08

PAGE 10

PAGE 12

PAGE 16

PAGE 20

PAGE 24

PAGE 26

TABLE OF CONTENTS

INTRODUCTION

SEEING STARS

When choosing a recipe, let the stars be your guide! Just follow this chart to find recipes that fit your cooking comfort level.

EASY: ★ ☆ ☆
MEDIUM: ★ ★ ☆
ADVANCED: ★ ★ ★

If you think vegetarian food is all about vegetables, think again. Sure vegetarians eat a lot of veggies, but they also enjoy pizza, peanut butter, pasta, and more. In fact, they pretty much eat everything except meat.

Are you a vegetarian or thinking about becoming one? Maybe you're just looking for fun and healthy recipes. Whatever your reason for picking up this book, you're sure to find delicious, meatless recipes.

METRIC CONVERSION GUIDE

United States	Metric
¼ teaspoon	1.2 mL
½ teaspoon	2.5 mL
1 teaspoon	5 mL
1 tablespoon	15 mL
¼ cup	60 mL
⅓ cup	80 mL
½ cup	120 mL
⅔ cup	160 mL
¾ cup	175 mL
1 cup	240 mL
1 quart	1 liter
1 ounce	30 grams
2 ounces	55 grams
4 ounces	110 grams
½ pound	225 grams
1 pound	455 grams

Fahrenheit	Celsius
325°	160°
350°	180°
375°	190°
400°	200°
425°	220°
450°	230°

All good cooks know that a successful recipe takes a little preparation. Use this handy checklist to save time when working in the kitchen.

BEFORE YOU BEGIN

READ YOUR RECIPE

Once you've chosen a recipe, carefully read over it. Everything will go smoothly if you understand the steps and techniques.

CHECK THE PANTRY

Make sure you have all the ingredients on hand. After all, it's hard to bake cookies without sugar!

DRESS FOR SUCCESS

Wear an apron to keep your clothes clean. Roll up long sleeves. Tie long hair back so it doesn't get in your way — or in the food.

GET OUT YOUR TOOLS

Sort through the cupboards and gather all the tools you'll need to prepare the recipe. Can't tell a spatula from a mixing spoon? No problem. Refer to the handy tools glossary in this book.

PREPARE YOUR INGREDIENTS

A little prep time at the start will pay off in the end.

- Rinse any fresh ingredients such as fruit and vegetables.
- Use a peeler to remove the peel from foods like apples and carrots.
- Cut up fresh ingredients as called for in the recipe. Keep an adult nearby when using a knife to cut or chop food.
- Measure all the ingredients and place them in separate bowls or containers so they're ready to use. Remember to use the correct measuring cups for dry and wet ingredients.

PREHEAT THE OVEN

If you're baking treats, it's important to preheat the oven. Cakes, cookies, and breads bake better in an oven that's heated to the correct temperature.

The kitchen may be unfamiliar turf for many young chefs. Here's a list of trusty tips to help keep you safe in the kitchen.

KITCHEN SAFETY

ADULT HELPERS

Ask an adult to help. Whether you're chopping, mixing, or baking, you'll want an adult nearby to lend a hand or answer questions.

FIRST AID

Keep a first aid kit handy in the kitchen, just in case you have an accident. A basic first aid kit contains bandages, a cream or spray to treat burns, alcohol wipes, gauze, and a small scissors.

WASH UP

Before starting any recipe, be sure to wash your hands. Wash your hands again after working with messy ingredients like jelly or syrup.

HANDLE HABITS

Turn handles of cooking pots toward the center of the stove. You don't want anyone to bump into a handle that's sticking off the stove.

USING KNIVES

It's always best to get an adult's help when using knives. Choose a knife that's the right size for your hands and the food. Hold the handle firmly when cutting, and keep your fingers away from the blade.

COVER UP

Always wear oven mitts or use pot holders to take hot trays and pans out of the oven.

KEEP IT CLEAN

Spills and drips are bound to happen in the kitchen. Wipe up messes with a paper towel or clean kitchen towel to keep your workspace tidy.

What happens when you mix pizza and grilled cheese? You get a Grilled Pizza Sandwich. What could be better for a quick meal or filling snack?

DIFFICULTY LEVEL: ★ ★ ☆
SERVING SIZE: 1

GRILLED PIZZA SANDWICH

WHAT YOU NEED

●● Ingredients

2 tablespoons butter
2 slices of bread
4 fresh basil leaves
1 roma tomato
2 mushrooms
2 tablespoons meatless pizza sauce
¼ cup shredded mozzarella cheese

●● Tools

butter knife   cutting board

paring knife   rubber scraper

skillet   spatula

1 With a butter knife, butter both slices of bread.

2 On a cutting board, cut basil into small pieces with a paring knife.

3 Cut tomato and mushrooms into thin slices with the paring knife.

4 With a rubber scraper, spread pizza sauce over the unbuttered side of one slice of bread.

5 Layer basil, tomato, mushrooms, and cheese over pizza sauce. Place the other slice of bread on top, buttered side up.

6 In a skillet, cook sandwich on medium-low heat for 4 minutes, until golden brown.

7 Use a spatula to flip the sandwich over. Cook an additional 4 minutes. Let sandwich cool for a few minutes before eating. Filling will be hot.

8

Pizza Party

Try this recipe at your next party. Just set up a pizza sandwich bar. All you need are the basic ingredients. Set out bread, sauce, cheese, basil, tomatoes, mushrooms, and any other tasty toppings you like on pizza. Let everybody pick what they want on their sandwiches. Then fry up personalized snacks.

Tired of eating cereal for breakfast every morning? Fruity Kebobs are just as easy to make, and they're full of flavor. For more fruity fun, dunk your fruit in the yogurt dip.

DIFFICULTY LEVEL: ★ ☆ ☆
SERVING SIZE: 2

FRUITY KEBOBS

WHAT YOU NEED

Ingredients

1 cup vanilla yogurt
3 tablespoons orange marmalade
1 tablespoon powdered sugar
1 kiwi
1 can pineapple chunks
1 can mandarin oranges
1 cup raspberries

Tools

small bowl

mixing spoon

cutting board

paring knife

colander

wooden skewers

1 To make the dip, add yogurt, marmalade, and powdered sugar to a small bowl. Stir ingredients together with a mixing spoon.

2 On a cutting board, use a paring knife to remove skin from kiwi. Cut kiwi into small pieces.

3 Drain pineapple and mandarin oranges into a colander.

4 Push a piece of kiwi onto a skewer. Then add a piece of pineapple, a mandarin orange, and a raspberry.

5 Continue adding fruit until the skewer is full. Repeat with remaining skewers until fruit is gone. Serve with yogurt dip.

11

Tasty Tip

These kebobs can be made using almost any fruity combination. Try cantalope, watermelon, and strawberries. For tropical fruit kebobs, use pineapple, mango, and bananas. Maybe you prefer apples, pears, and peaches. See what fun creations you can come up with.

A great salad doesn't always mean a bowl full of lettuce. This Spaghetti Salad doesn't have any lettuce at all. It's a tasty mix of veggies and pasta.

SPAGHETTI SALAD

WHAT YOU NEED

•• *Ingredients*

1 (12-ounce) package spaghetti noodles
1 cup shredded mozzarella cheese
1 (14.5-ounce) can diced tomatoes
1 (2-ounce) can sliced black olives
1 teaspoon onion powder
1 teaspoon garlic powder
1 cup Italian salad dressing

•• *Tools*

saucepan

colander

mixing bowl

mixing spoon

1 In a large saucepan, cook noodles according to package directions. Drain cooked noodles in a colander. Rinse with cold water and set aside.

2 In a mixing bowl, add cheese, tomatoes, black olives, onion powder, and garlic powder.

3 Add spaghetti to the mixing bowl. Drizzle with salad dressing.

4 Toss ingredients together lightly with a mixing spoon.

5 Refrigerate for 1 hour before serving.

Tasty Tip

Spaghetti Salad is the perfect food for experimenting because there are so many ways to make it. For extra flavor, add chopped green peppers, mushrooms, or cucumber. If you don't have spaghetti noodles, try this recipe with corkscrew pasta or penne pasta.

When you want an afterschool snack, tofu may not be your first thought. But these Tofu Nuggets are full of protein, so you'll have plenty of energy to finish your homework.

DIFFICULTY LEVEL: ★ ★ ★
SERVING SIZE: 2-3
PREHEAT OVEN: 350° FAHRENHEIT

TOFU NUGGETS

WHAT YOU NEED

●● Ingredients

¼ cup milk
2 tablespoons mustard
1 teaspoon salt
½ teaspoon pepper
1 teaspoon onion powder
1 teaspoon garlic powder
1 cup breadcrumbs
1 block extra firm tofu

●● Tools

small bowl   whisk   mixing bowl

cutting board   paring knife   baking sheet

oven mitt   pot holder   spatula

paper towel

1 In a small bowl, combine milk and mustard with a whisk.

2 In a mixing bowl, stir together salt, pepper, onion powder, garlic powder, and breadcrumbs.

3 Wrap tofu in a paper towel and squeeze out the extra water. On a cutting board, cut tofu into chunks with a paring knife.

4 Dip each piece of tofu into the milk mixture. Roll tofu in the breadcrumb mixture until covered.

5 Place tofu on a baking sheet. Bake for 15 minutes. Use oven mitts or pot holders to remove baking sheet from the oven. Use a spatula to flip over each piece.

6 Return baking sheet to the oven and bake an additional 10 minutes.

7 Use oven mitts or pot holders to remove baking sheet from the oven. Allow nuggets to cool for 5 minutes. Serve with barbecue sauce or honey.

Tofu For You

Meat is filled with protein. Vegetarians don't eat meat, so they need to find other protein sources. Tofu is a popular choice. It is made from soybeans and comes in many different forms and textures. Extra firm tofu, which is used in this recipe, holds its shape well. Silken tofu is creamy and can be used to make soft foods like pudding. Experiment with the different types of tofu to find your favorite.

When you don't have time to make a big meal, try making this Pita Pocket Salad. You don't need a fork, so it's great when you're on the go.

PITA POCKET SALAD

WHAT YOU NEED

●● *Ingredients*

6 grape or cherry tomatoes
1 pita
1 cup shredded lettuce
1 cup shredded carrots
1 cup shredded cheddar cheese
4 tablespoons salad dressing
    (ranch or Caesar works well)

●● *Tools*

cutting board

paring knife

1 On a cutting board, cut tomatoes in half with a paring knife.

2 Cut pita in half.

3 Open one pita pocket and add half of the lettuce, carrots, tomatoes, and cheese.

4 Drizzle 2 tablespoons salad dressing on top.

5 Open the other pita pocket. Repeat steps 3 and 4 with remaining ingredients.

Eat a Pita

Pita bread is a round, flat bread that forms a pocket during baking. It is especially popular in Greece, where they use the bread to wrap gyros or kebabs. Pita bread is also a traditional food in the Middle East, the Mediterranean, and North Africa.

17

Tell Mom you'll make dinner tonight. This cheesy casserole is a fun and easy way to feed your whole family.

EASY CHEESY POTATOES

WHAT YOU NEED

●● Ingredients

1 (32-ounce) bag tater tots
1 (10-ounce) can cream of mushroom soup
1 teaspoon pepper
1 (16-ounce) container sour cream
2 cups shredded cheese
    (Monterey Jack and cheddar)

●● Tools

9 x 13 baking pan   mixing bowl

rubber scraper   oven mitt

pot holder

nonstick cooking spray

1 Remove tater tots from the freezer. Allow to thaw for 20–30 minutes.

2 Spray baking pan with nonstick cooking spray.

3 Place tater tots in a mixing bowl.

4 Add soup, pepper, sour cream, and half of the cheese to the mixing bowl. Stir ingredients together with a rubber scraper.

5 Pour mixture into the casserole dish. Sprinkle remaining cheese on top.

6 Bake for 45 minutes. Use oven mitts or pot holders to remove dish from oven. Allow to cool for 5–10 minutes before serving.

More Cheese Please

Cheese is a great source of calcium. Calcium keeps your bones and teeth healthy. Everyone should eat three servings of calcium-rich foods each day. Other great sources of calcium include yogurt and milk.

Invite some friends over for a Mexican fiesta. Decorate with tissue paper flowers, and serve this traditional Mexican dish.

DIFFICULTY LEVEL: ★ ★ ☆
SERVING SIZE: 6
PREHEAT OVEN: 350° FAHRENHEIT

BEAN BURRITO BAKE

WHAT YOU NEED

• • Ingredients

2 (16-ounce) cans refried beans
6 (10-inch) flour tortillas
1 cup salsa
1 cup sour cream
2 cups shredded cheese
    (cheddar or Monterey Jack works well)

• • Tools

9 x 13 baking pan   rubber scraper

oven mitt   pot holder

tablespoon

nonstick cooking spray
aluminum foil

1 Spray a 9 x 13 baking pan with nonstick cooking spray.

2 With a rubber scraper, spread an equal amount of refried beans on each tortilla.

3 Add 2 tablespoons of salsa and sour cream to each tortilla.

4 Sprinkle 1 cup cheese equally over the tortillas.

5 Roll up each burrito and place in the baking pan with the fold side down. Sprinkle remaining cheese on top of the burritos.

6 Cover the baking pan with aluminum foil and bake for 20 minutes.

7 Use oven mitts or pot holders to remove pan from oven. Carefully remove the aluminum foil. Bake an additional 5 minutes. Use oven mitts or pot holders to remove pan from the oven.

8 Just before serving, top each burrito with a spoonful of sour cream.

What Are They?

Refried beans are a popular Mexican dish. They are made using either black beans or pinto beans. The beans are soaked in water overnight. Then they are boiled. After that, the beans are mashed and fried.

You don't need a bunch of ingredients to make a great meal.
Just a few ingredients pack a ton of flavor into this pasta dish.

PERFECT PASTA

WHAT YOU NEED

● ● *Ingredients*

2 cups penne pasta
2 cups chopped broccoli (fresh or frozen)
4 tablespoons butter
2 teaspoons garlic powder
1 teaspoon salt
1 teaspoon pepper
10 grape tomatoes
½ cup finely grated Parmesan cheese

● ● *Tools*

saucepan

colander

mixing spoon

1 In a large saucepan, cook pasta according to package directions. When 5 minutes remain in the cooking process, add broccoli to the water.

2 Drain cooked pasta and broccoli in a colander and set aside.

3 Return the saucepan to the stove. Add butter, garlic powder, salt, and pepper to the saucepan. Cook on low heat until butter melts.

4 Once butter melts, add tomatoes. Turn off the stove.

5 Return pasta and broccoli to the saucepan. Stir ingredients together with a mixing spoon.

6 Sprinkle Parmesan cheese on top of pasta just before serving.

Plenty of Pasta

The average person eats pasta once a week. For Americans, that adds up to 15 pounds of pasta each year. Italians eat pasta much more often. An average Italian eats 51 pounds of pasta each year.

How do you make a delicious meal even better? By serving a delicious dessert. With a combination of yogurt and fresh fruit, this pie is sure to please.

RASPBERRY CREAM PIE

WHAT YOU NEED

•• *Ingredients*

1 (8-ounce) container whipped topping
1¾ cups raspberry yogurt
1 graham cracker piecrust
½ cup fresh raspberries

•• *Tools*

mixing bowl

rubber scraper

1 In a mixing bowl, combine whipped topping and the yogurt with a rubber scraper.

2 Pour yogurt mix into the piecrust.

3 Place pie in freezer for 2½–3 hours.

4 Take pie out of the freezer 5 minutes before serving. Decorate the top of the pie with raspberries and whipped topping.

Tasty Tip

Dress up your pie by transforming it into a Mixed Berry Cream Pie. Along with the raspberries, add ½ cup blueberries and ½ cup blackberries to step 4. Try substituting blueberry or vanilla yogurt for the raspberry yogurt.

25

Peanut butter and jelly sandwiches are nothing new. But make them into muffins, and everyone will want to trade lunches with you.

DIFFICULTY LEVEL: ★ ★ ☆
SERVING SIZE: 12
PREHEAT OVEN: 350° FAHRENHEIT

PEANUT BUTTER AND JELLY MUFFINS

WHAT YOU NEED

●● Ingredients

1¾ cups flour
⅔ cup brown sugar
2½ teaspoons baking powder
1 egg
¾ cup milk
⅔ cup chunky peanut butter
¼ cup vegetable oil
2 teaspoons vanilla extract
strawberry or grape jelly

●● Tools

baking cups

muffin pan

2 mixing bowls

rubber scraper

oven mitt

pot holder

1 Put baking cups into a muffin pan.

2 In a mixing bowl, combine flour, brown sugar, and baking powder with a rubber scraper.

3 Crack egg into a second mixing bowl and throw away shell.

4 Add milk, peanut butter, oil, and vanilla to the second mixing bowl. Mix ingredients together.

5 Stir flour mixture into the egg mixture.

6 Spoon batter into the baking cups, filling each ⅓ full. Scoop a teaspoon of jelly into each cup. Add more batter until each cup is ⅔ full.

7 Bake for 15–17 minutes. Use oven mitts or pot holders to remove pan from oven. Allow muffins to cool for 10 minutes before serving.

TOOLS GLOSSARY

9 x 13 baking pan — a glass or metal pan used to cook food

baking cups — disposable paper or foil cups that are placed into a muffin pan to keep batter from sticking to the pan

baking sheet — a flat, metal tray used for baking foods

butter knife — an eating utensil often used to spread ingredients

colander — a bowl-shaped strainer used for washing or draining food

cutting board — a wooden or plastic board used when slicing or chopping foods

mixing bowl — a sturdy bowl used for mixing ingredients

mixing spoon — a large spoon with a wide circular end used to mix ingredients

muffin pan — a pan with individual cups for baking cupcakes or muffins

oven mitt — a large mitten made from heavy fabric used to protect hands when removing hot pans from the oven

paring knife — a small, sharp knife used for peeling or slicing

pot holder — a thick, heavy fabric cut into a square or circle that is used to remove hot pans from an oven

rubber scraper — a kitchen tool with a rubber paddle on one end

small bowl — a bowl used for mixing a small amount of ingredients

whisk — a metal tool used for beating ingredients

saucepan — a deep pot used for stovetop cooking

spatula — a kitchen tool with a broad, flat, metal or plastic blade at the end, used for removing foods from the pans

wooden skewers — long sticks used to hold pieces of food together

skillet — a flat pan used to cook non-liquid foods on a stovetop

tablespoon — an eating utensil often used to stir or scoop

GLOSSARY

drizzle (DRIZ-uhl) — to let a substance fall in small drops, like a light rain

fiesta (fee-ESS-tuh) — a holiday or religious festival, especially in Spanish-speaking countries

gyro (YEE-roh) — a Greek sandwich made with meat, vegetables, yogurt sauce, and pita bread

kebob (ke-BAHB) — layered foods held together with a thin stick

protein (PROH-teen) — a substance found in foods such as meat, cheese, eggs, and fish

tofu (TOH-foo) — a soft, cheese-like food made from soybeans

vegetarian (vej-uh-TER-ee-uhn) — someone who does not eat meat

Bojang, Ali Brownlie. *Why Are People Vegetarian?* Exploring Tough Issues. Austin, Texas: Raintree, 2002.

Gillies, Judi, and Jennifer Glossop. *The Jumbo Vegetarian Cookbook.* Tonawanda, N.Y.: Kids Can Press, 2002.

Mattare, Marty, and Wendy Muldawer. *Better Than Peanut Butter & Jelly: Quick Vegetarian Meals Your Kids Will Love.* Ithaca, N.Y.: McBooks Press, 2006.

McCann, Jennifer. *Vegan Lunch Box: 150 Amazing, Animal-free Lunches Kids and Grown-ups Will Love.* Cambridge, Mass., Da Capo Press, 2008.

FactHound offers a safe, fun way to find Internet sites related to this book. All of the sites on FactHound have been researched by our staff.

Here's how:
1. Visit *www.facthound.com*
2. Choose your grade level.
3. Type in this book ID **1429620188** for age-appropriate sites. You may also browse subjects by clicking on letters, or by clicking on pictures and words.
4. Click on the **Fetch It** button.

FactHound will fetch the best sites for you!

ABOUT THE AUTHOR

Kristi Johnson got her start in the kitchen when she was a little girl helping her mom, aunt, and grandmas with cooking and baking. Over the years, she decided that her true passion was in baking. She spent many days in the kitchen covering every countertop with her favorite chocolate chip cookies. Kristi attended the baking program at the Le Cordon Bleu College of Culinary Arts in Minnesota. After graduating with highest honors, Kristi worked in many restaurants and currently works in the baking industry.

INDEX